EVERYDAY SCIENCE

at the seaside

Barbara Taylor

photography by
Peter Millard

MACDONALD YOUNG BOOKS

First published in 1995
by Macdonald Young
Books Ltd
Campus 400
Maylands Avenue
Hemel Hempstead
Hertfordshire HP2 7EZ

Text © Barbara Taylor 1995

Illustration © Macdonald Young Books Ltd 1995

Commissioning editor: Debbie Fox

Project editor: Caroline Wilson

Design: The Design Works, Reading

Illustrators: Kevin Jones Associates,
David Pattison

The publisher and author would like to thank
Carol Olivier of Kenmont Primary School, and
the following children for taking part in the
photography: Jetro Boylan, Marissa Clarke,
Sandra Gaspar, Robert Hazell, Rhomaine
Hewitt, Lauren Samuels, Sabrina Shanghanoo
and Samantha Wallace.

Thanks also to Elaine Tanner, Wendy Bray and
Angela Bickerton and their classes at St James'
Primary School.

Printed and bound in Portugal by Edições ASA

A CIP catalogue record for this book is
available from the British Library.

ISBN 0 7500 1754 6

Contents

Seaside code

- Wear shoes that will not slip on wet rocks.
- If you go into the water, make sure an adult is with you.
- Don't swim near boats, surfers or windsurfers.
- It is safest not to play with inflatable rings, air beds or toy boats. You could quickly be taken out to sea.
- Try not to disturb beach animals and always put them back where you find them.

Why do I get a suntan on the beach?

Your skin goes darker so that the sun will not damage it. This happens even if you have a black or brown skin to start with. In hot sun, your skin makes more of a dark substance called melanin, which soaks up the harmful rays of the sun and stops you burning. But it takes several days for your skin to do this. So if you get too much hot sun too quickly, your skin may burn.

How the skin tans

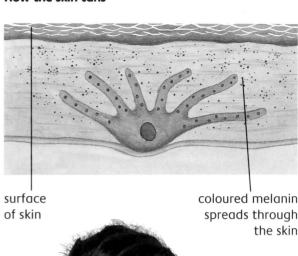

surface of skin

coloured melanin spreads through the skin

Why do people with fair skins burn easily?

People with fair skins make less melanin in their skin, so they have less protection from the sun. If they sit out in hot sun for too long, tiny tubes in the skin swell up and fill with blood. Their skin becomes red and sore.

Did you know that dogs have no sweat glands, so they cannot sweat to cool down? Panting helps them to cool down because water escapes from the tongue, taking heat away with it.

Why do I put on suncream?

Suncream protects you by blocking out harmful rays from the sun. This gives you time to build up a protective layer of melanin in your skin. Suncream comes in different strengths, called factors. People with sensitive skins need high factor numbers, such as 15, or even 25.

Why do I need to wear a sunhat?

A sunhat keeps your head cool, which helps to stop you feeling dizzy or sick or even getting sunstroke. It also helps to keep the sun out of your eyes. Strong sunlight can damage your eyes. Some sunglasses also block out the sun's harmful rays.

Very small babies need to be kept out of hot sun because they cannot control the temperature of their bodies very well. This means they can get overheated easily. Babies also have very sensitive skin and burn more quickly than older children.

The wind rolls larger grains of sand along the beach. It blows smaller grains along in a series of jumps, rather like a relay race. When one grain falls, it may hit another, making it bounce up into the air. This is called saltation.

Why is it often windy near the sea?

The sea warms up and cools down more slowly than the land. On a clear, hot day, the sun heats up the seashore and warm air above the shore rises up into the sky. Cooler air from over the sea is drawn in to take its place. This means that a nice cool breeze blows on to the beach.

Why does sand get in my eyes on a windy day?

The tiny grains of sand on a beach are light enough to be picked up by the wind. They swirl along the beach and can scratch the delicate surfaces of your eyes. Blinking helps to keep out the gritty grains, and your eyes may water to wash away the sand.

Did you know that the windiest place in the world is the George Fifth Coast in Antarctica? Winds there often blow at 320 kph, that's over three times as fast as the average car – or average cheetah!

Why is the beach a good place to fly my kite?

Kites need the wind to push them up into the air. If you run along the beach holding your kite, you make the air move over and under the kite. Air moving over the kite presses on it less than air flowing underneath it. The greater air pressure below the kite helps the wind to push the kite up off the ground. Some kites need a tail to make them more stable and keep them in the right position for the wind.

True or false?

1 A Thai snake kite was 24 times longer than one of the longest dinosaurs, *Diplodocus.*

2 A refreshing sea breeze in Fremantle, Australia, is called the 'doctor'.

3 The wind may blow the sand on the beach into sand dunes as tall as skyscrapers.

The answers are on page 32.

What sort of sand is best for building my sandcastle?

Damp sand sticks together well and can be moulded into different shapes using your hands, buckets or sand moulds. But if the sand is too wet, the towers of a sandcastle soon collapse. Fine, damp sand is best for sandcastles. Water in the little spaces between the grains 'sticks' the sand together like glue. This is called cohesion. It's impossible to make a sandcastle with very dry sand, it just crumbles away before your eyes.

Did you know that one sandcastle contains millions of grains of sand?

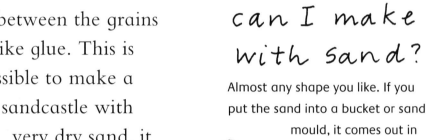

What shapes can I make with sand?

Almost any shape you like. If you put the sand into a bucket or sand mould, it comes out in the shape of the container. You need to press it down firmly to 'stick' the sand grains together well. You can also make cars or boats out of sand, or even bury your family or friends!

Did you know that some artists make huge sand sculptures on the beach? They can build life-size sand horses galloping into the waves.

The female loggerhead turtle swims ashore at night and digs a deep hole in the beach sand to lay her eggs. She lays about 100 eggs at a time.

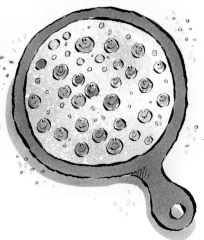

What is sand made of?

Sand is made up of tiny bits of rocks, shells, fish skeletons and coral ground up by the sea. Yellow sand contains quartz, pink or white sand contains coral, and black sand contains volcanic rock or coal.

Why do my feet sink into the sand?

The weight of your body pushes down through your feet, creating a big pushing force over a small area. This is called high pressure. In dry sand, your feet push the grains aside, making a dip which you sink into. Walking is hard work in this sort of sand. On wet sand, the pressure of your feet squeezes out the water between the grains, leaving a footprint full of water.

9

What lives under the sand?

It often looks as if there are no animals on a sandy beach, but buried in the sand are animals such as worms, shellfish, sea urchins and crabs. The sand protects these animals from waves, enemies, sunshine and cold. You may see little holes and dents in the sand where the animals are hiding beneath. If you dig in the sand near the sea, where it is wetter, you will find more animals near the surface.

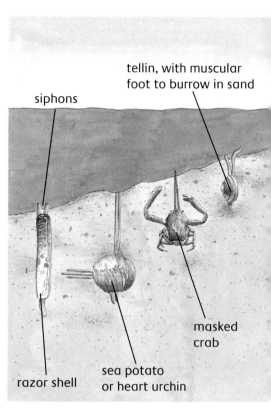

tellin, with muscular foot to burrow in sand

siphons

masked crab

razor shell

sea potato or heart urchin

Did you know that a razor shell can dig down into the sand faster than a person?

How do animals breathe under the sand?

The animals have different ways of drawing seawater into their bodies. Then they take oxygen gas from the water. Razor shells and tellins suck in seawater through long tubes called siphons. Sea potatoes dig a tunnel through the sand to reach the water. And the masked crab zips its feelers together and sticks them out into the water.

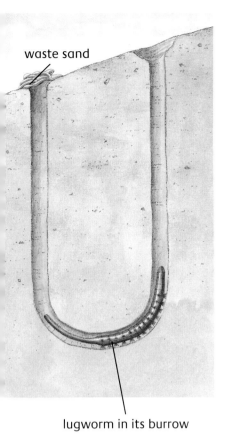

waste sand

lugworm in its burrow

What are the sandy squiggles on the beach?

Lugworms live under the sand in U-shaped burrows. They swallow sand and mud, taking in food from them. Then they squirt waste sand and mud out of the other end of the burrow, rather like squeezing toothpaste out of a tube! The waste piles up into little squiggly heaps. Lugworms have soft bodies and living in the sand helps to protect them from enemies.

Why can I hear the sea in a shell?

The swishing sound you hear when you hold a shell to your ear is not the sea at all. It is the sound of your own blood rushing through tubes inside your ear. The shell makes the sound louder because it is bouncing around inside a small space.

Can you guess...?

Which animals made these tracks in the sand?

The answers are on page 32.

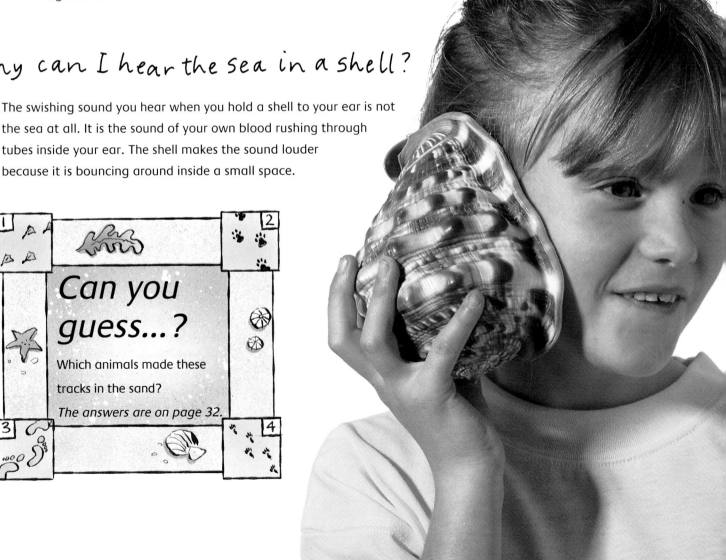

Why are pebbles so smooth?

As pieces of rock roll around in the sea, the edges rub against each other. The rough corners are eventually worn away, leaving smooth, round pebbles. Sometimes, a piece of rock has a crack or a weak point and the sea eats into the stone, making a hole in it.

little tern's egg

Birds that nest on rocky shores have eggs with spotty patterns that match the beach background. Ringed plover or little tern eggs are hard for enemies to spot against a background of pebbles This is called camouflage.

Why are pebbles different shapes?

It all depends on the sort of rock they are made of. Very hard rocks like granite produce ball-shaped pebbles. Rocks that naturally split into slabs, such as slate, produce flatter, disc-shaped pebbles.

Why are some beaches pebbly?

When the sea pounds against a rocky shore, it breaks off pieces of rock. These eventually wear away to form pebbles. Large pebbles break up into smaller ones and eventually turn into shingle. After a long time, the bits become so small, they make sand.

Where can I find treasure on the beach?

The sea sometimes washes up pieces of semi-precious stones such as jet, jasper, amethyst, agate or garnet, which make up some of the pebbles. And pieces of coloured glass look like treasure. So it's worth keeping a sharp look-out on a pebble beach.

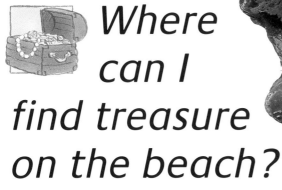

Did you know that some insects were trapped in the sticky sap oozing out of trees millions of years ago? Today, the sap has set hard, like toffee, to form amber. You may find pieces of amber on the beach.

Shells sometimes have holes in them as well. The large necklace shell bores holes through the shells of other shellfish to eat the soft body of the animal inside.

hole made by necklace shell

necklace shell

Why do crabs have pincers?

Crabs use their big front pincers, or claws, for picking up, cutting and crushing their food. Sharp, wavy edges help with grasping slippery food and cutting it up. Crabs may also use their pincers to defend themselves, sometimes nipping people's toes! Male crabs wave their claws to threaten rivals or impress a mate.

Did you know that pea crabs are the smallest crabs in the world? They live and feed inside the shells of scallops, oysters and mussels. Their shells are about the size of a pea.

Hermit crabs take over the empty shells of other sea creatures to live in. The shell protects the soft back part of their body. As a hermit crab grows bigger, it changes its borrowed shell for a larger one.

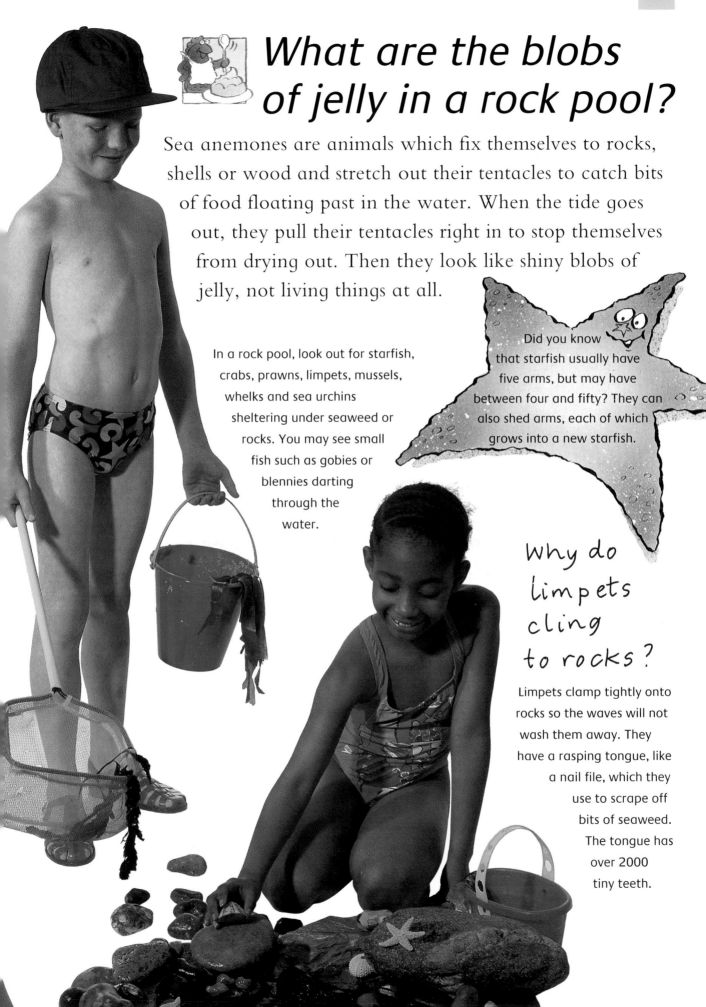

What are the blobs of jelly in a rock pool?

Sea anemones are animals which fix themselves to rocks, shells or wood and stretch out their tentacles to catch bits of food floating past in the water. When the tide goes out, they pull their tentacles right in to stop themselves from drying out. Then they look like shiny blobs of jelly, not living things at all.

In a rock pool, look out for starfish, crabs, prawns, limpets, mussels, whelks and sea urchins sheltering under seaweed or rocks. You may see small fish such as gobies or blennies darting through the water.

Did you know that starfish usually have five arms, but may have between four and fifty? They can also shed arms, each of which grows into a new starfish.

Why do limpets cling to rocks?

Limpets clamp tightly onto rocks so the waves will not wash them away. They have a rasping tongue, like a nail file, which they use to scrape off bits of seaweed. The tongue has over 2000 tiny teeth.

Why can I often see rainbow colours on shells?

The beautiful shiny colours are caused by the way light is reflected between the thin layers of the shell. Sunlight is really made up of all the colours of the rainbow. The shell separates out all these colours so we can see each one by itself. These colours are called iridescent, which means they shine when they catch the light.

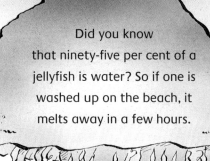

Did you know that ninety-five per cent of a jellyfish is water? So if one is washed up on the beach, it melts away in a few hours.

Why are some shells joined together?

One group of shellfish have their shells divided into two parts or valves. They are called bivalves, meaning two valves. Clams are bivalves, so are scallops, mussels and tellins. The two valves are joined together by a ridge or teeth that form a hinge. Bivalves open their valves to feed.

mussel

scallop

ormer shell

Why is seaweed slippery and slimy?

Seaweed has a coating that stops it taking in too much seawater and getting waterlogged. It also helps to stop the plant drying out if it is exposed to the air. You can hang seaweed up and use it to help you forecast the weather. If rain is on the way, the seaweed takes in moisture from the air and feels damp.

True or false?

1 Goose barnacles live on the feet of geese.

2 A mermaid's purse contains gold.

3 A sea urchin's skeleton is called a test.

4 Coconuts float across the sea to find new beaches to live on.

The answers are on page 32.

Why does some seaweed pop under my feet?

Your feet squash the little bags full of air that help the seaweed to float in the sea. The air escapes with a pop!

The water in a wave stays in more or less the same place. It moves around in circles. Near the beach, the sea is too shallow for the water to make a complete circle. So the top of the wave curves over and the wave breaks.

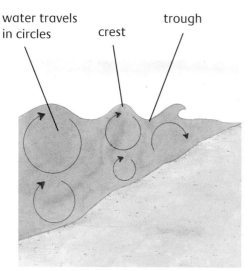

water travels in circles

crest

trough

Where do waves come from?

The wind makes the waves. As the wind blows over the surface of the oceans, it pushes and drags the water into ripples or waves. The size of a wave depends on the speed of the wind and how long and how far the wind has been blowing. Waves usually travel in straight lines. They can travel for many hours across the open ocean before they reach the shore.

How do malibu surfers ride a wall of water?

Surfers hitch a ride on huge waves about to break on the shore. They stand on the crest of the wave and use the force of gravity to ride down the wall of water, travelling faster than the wave, at up to 15 kph. Surfers have to try and stay just ahead of the breaking crest of the wave.

Why does the sea move up and down the beach?

On most beaches, the sea moves up and down the beach twice a day. This movement is called the tide and it is caused by an invisible pulling force called gravity. Big things have a bigger gravity than smaller ones. The earth, the sun and the moon are very big indeed, and their gravity is also huge. When the gravity of the sun and of the moon tugs at the earth's oceans, this produces the tides.

Did you know that the greatest tides happen in the Bay of Fundy, Canada? They can rise over 15 m, higher than a four-storey building, in just six hours.

What are spring tides?

When the sun and the moon are in a straight line with the earth, they pull extra hard. This causes very high and very low tides, called spring tides. They happen every two weeks and have nothing to do with the season called spring.

Sea snakes can stay underwater for up to eight hours because most of their body is a huge lung, which stores oxygen. The snakes have to come to the surface to breathe air.

How do my armbands help me to float?

Armbands help you to float while you are learning to swim. The air inside them is lighter than water, so they hold you up on the surface. This stops you sinking down through the water. It is quite hard to sink in the sea, because the salty water is heavier, or more dense, than fresh water. It pushes up strongly against your body, helping you to float easily.

Why do flippers help me swim fast

Flippers help you to swim fast because their big flaps are much better at pushing against the water than your feet. They are like the webbed feet of seabirds, such as gulls.

How does my snorkel work?

A snorkel is a bent tube which lets you breathe air while your face is under the water. You put one end in your mouth and keep the top of the tube sticking out of the water. So you can swim around looking for fish without coming up for air. If you dive down, your snorkel fills up with water and you have to hold your breath. Next time you come to the surface, you blow out the water and the snorkel is ready to use again.

In warm, shallow seas, you may be able to swim over a coral reef with a snorkel. Coral reefs are built up from the skeletons of tiny animals called corals. They take thousands of years to form.

Did you know that the bikini is named after the two-piece clothing worn by women on the coral island of Bikini in the South Pacific?

Why can't I breathe under water?

When you breathe air, you take in a gas called oxygen. You need this oxygen to stay alive because oxygen sets free energy from your food. Oxygen is also in water but your body isn't designed for getting oxygen from water. If people need to stay underwater for a long time, they take tanks of oxygen with them.

Why does the sea taste salty?

The salt in the sea comes from rocks on the land. Rivers wash salts out of the rocks and into the sea. You can't see the salt in the sea, but you can taste it. If you lie in the sun to dry off after a swim, you may see a white powder on your skin. This is salt, left behind when the water turns into a gas and disappears into the air.

Did you know that people take enough salt from the sea each year to build the Great Pyramid in Egypt just out of salt – about six million tonnes?

Why is the sea blue?

When light falls on the sea, some of the blue or green light bounces back from bits of sand, salt and other things in the water. This makes the sea look blue or green if you are sitting on the beach. The other colours in the sunlight are taken in, or absorbed, by the seawater.

Why is the sea chilly early in the year?

In summer, the sea warms up as it absorbs heat from the sun. But in spring, the sea takes longer to warm up than the land, so it often feels chilly. Seawater needs five times as much heat to raise its temperature as the same weight of rock. So even though the beach may be warm early in the year, the sea may be cold.

Did you know that animals that swim in freezing seas, such as polar bears, whales or penguins, have very thick layers of fat under their skin? This fat is called blubber and it keeps the animals warm.

Why do I feel cold in the sea?

Children get colder more quickly than adults because they have less body fat. The fat helps to stop the heat of the body escaping. Don't stay in the sea if you feel cold. When you come out, it's not a good idea to rub your body with a towel. This brings blood to the surface of the skin, taking blood away from your heart, lungs and other important organs inside your body. Just wrap a towel around you and get dressed as soon as you can.

Why does my ice cream melt?

The heat from the air, and from your hands, makes the solid ice cream melt and go runny. Heat often changes things in this way. When the ice cream warms up, the particles it is made of move about more. The ice cream can't hold its shape very easily, so it collapses and melts.

Did you know that clever Japanese monkeys called macaques sometimes wash sweet potatoes in the sea? They do this to make sure their food is clean before they eat it.

Why shouldn't I swim after lunch?

You may get cramp, which makes it dangerous to swim. After eating, a lot of blood is needed to help with digesting or breaking down your food. If you ask your muscles to do a lot of work in swimming, they will need extra blood as well, for energy. If your muscles do not get enough blood, they sometimes give you a painful cramp and stop working properly.

How does my coolbox keep things cool?

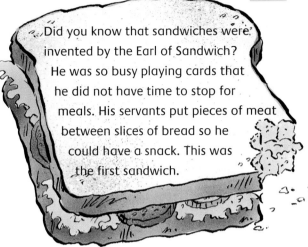

Did you know that sandwiches were invented by the Earl of Sandwich? He was so busy playing cards that he did not have time to stop for meals. His servants put pieces of meat between slices of bread so he could have a snack. This was the first sandwich.

A coolbox is made of a material that stops heat getting into the box from outside. Materials that do not carry heat easily are called insulating materials. When you put special freezer packs into the coolbox, your picnic keeps cool and fresh. Food may go bad if it is kept in a hot place all day, and things like chocolate will melt. Keeping your drinks cold is important too – they help you to cool down on a hot day.

Where do the bubbles come from in fizzy drinks?

The bubbles in fizzy drinks are made of a gas called carbon dioxide. The gas is squashed into the bottle or can so hard that it disappears into the drink. The bubbles escape when you open the can or bottle.

Why does my soft tennis ball go slowly?

Did you know that windsurfers can zoom over the sea at up to 50 kph – as fast as a car?

The spongy tennis balls used for soft tennis have a rough surface. This catches against the air because of a force called friction, which slows down the ball so it doesn't fly through the air too fast. This is why soft tennis is ideal for playing on crowded beaches. Because plastic tennis rackets have hard strings, they don't hit the ball very far. Real tennis rackets have bendy, elastic strings which push the ball through the air much faster.

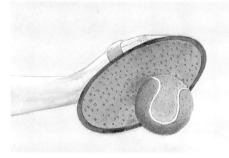

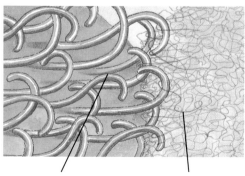

hooks on bat   hairy ball

Why do scatchball bats stop the ball in mid-air?

One side of the bat is covered in tiny hooks which catch the extra hairy surface of the ball, stopping it dead in its tracks. The two rough surfaces meeting each other create a high sticking force, or high friction.

How does a windsurfer glide over the sea?

The person on a windsurfer pulls and pushes on a bar to move the sail around the mast. They use the sail to catch the wind, no matter which direction the wind is blowing from. The wind fills up the sail and drives the board along. The sail is also used to steer the windsurfer.

wind

wind pushes sail and drives board forwards

How do paragliders get off the ground?

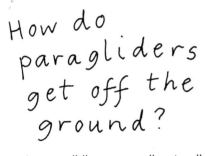

In paragliding, a speedboat pulls someone wearing skis along a platform. They are also attached to a parachute. Because the boat is moving quite fast, wind fills the parachute and lifts the person into the air. It works rather like a kite once it is off the ground.

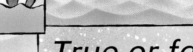
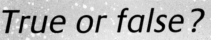

True or false?

1 Beach balls float because they are full of water.

2 Some people can water-ski on their bare feet, without using any skis.

3 Canoes are usually red underneath so fish can see them coming.

4 The best surfing waves are up to 9 m high and occur in Hawaii, Australia and Bali.

The answers are on page 32.

Why do I sometimes get tar on my feet?

Oil from oil tankers may escape into the sea if there is an accident on an oil rig or if the tanker hits a rock or another ship and sinks. Tankers may also wash out their tanks at sea, which means that waste oil gets into the water. Waves and tides bring the oil on to the beach where it dries out and collects in sticky black lumps called tar. Once this sticks to your feet or clothes, it is hard to clean off, except with eucalyptus oil or special tar remover.

The feet of people tramping over the dunes can wear them away. Planting marram grass on the dunes helps to keep them in place. The roots of the grass bind the sand together and stop the wind blowing it away.

Did you know that monk seals in the Mediterranean sea have been pushed off the beaches where they once raised their pups by tourists in search of the sun?

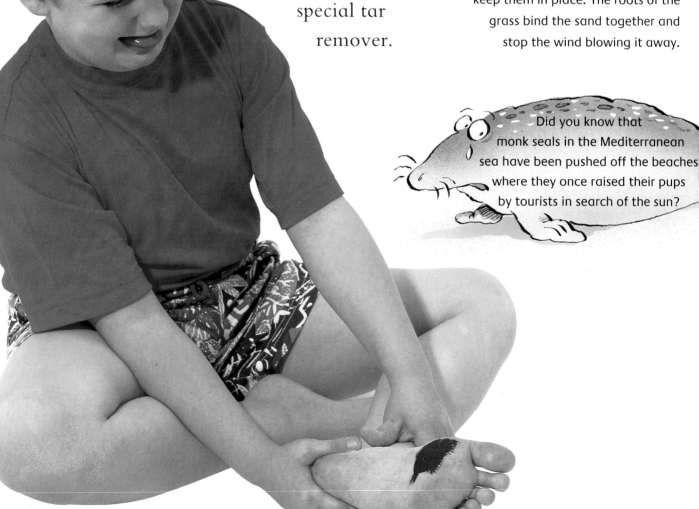

Why is there litter on some beaches?

People sometimes leave the remains of their picnic and other litter behind on the beach. As well as making the beach look unpleasant, litter can be dangerous. It can carry germs and diseases and make the sand or pebbles dirty. People and other animals may cut themselves on cans and broken glass. Small animals can also become trapped in bottles. Next time you go to the seaside, take your litter home with you. Then the beach will be cleaner and safer for people and wildlife.

Coral reefs are threatened by pollution, mining, people taking bits of coral for souvenirs, and tourists anchoring boats on reefs and walking over them. The coral is made up of living animals, and if it dies, so does the huge variety of life that lives on it.

Why is some seawater not safe to swim in?

On some beaches, sewage is pumped into the sea through long pipes. Although it is supposed to go far out to sea, some may be washed up on to the beach. Factory wastes and beach litter also make the water dirty. If seawater contains germs, you may be ill if you swim in it. Beaches often have signs to tell you how clean the water is.

More about seaside science

When you are playing on the beach, you are discovering all kinds of science – from floating, forces, waves and tides to how wildlife survives at the seaside. Across these two pages, you can read about some of the most important science ideas in this book.

1 The sun's rays that make you tan are called **ultraviolet rays**. High in the sky, the ozone layer stops too many of these rays getting through to the Earth.

2 **Melanin** is the brown dye in your skin that gives you a tan.

3 The force of air pressing up against a kite and keeping it up in the air is called **lift**.

The **wind** blows when air moves from place to place.

4 **Pressure** is the amount of force pushing down on a certain area.

5 A sticking force called **friction** happens when two surfaces rub against each other. Friction slows things down or stops them moving.

6 Most of the shells on the beach belong to a group of animals called **molluscs**. Mollusc shells protect the soft bodies of the animals inside. The shell may be made of one piece, like a snail – these are called **univalves**, meaning one valve. Or the shell may have two pieces, like a mussel – these are called **bivalves**, meaning two valves. Crabs also have shells, so do bird's eggs.

Birds that don't build nests often lay eggs with **camouflaged** markings that match the background.

7 **Iridescent** shells shine with rainbow colours when light is reflected from them.

8 The force that draws together particles of the same substance is called **cohesion**. Cohesive forces between water particles in damp sand stick a sandcastle together.

9 When you breathe, you take in a gas called **oxygen**. Inside your body, oxygen sets free energy from your food. Oxygen keeps you alive.

10 You float in the sea because the seawater pushes up against your body with a force called **upthrust**.

11 Waves **erode** the beach, breaking down rocks to form pebbles, then shingle, and finally sand.

The **tides** are caused by the **gravity** of the sun and moon, which pull the sea up and down the beach.

Gravity is an invisible pulling force that attracts one object to another.

12 Heat makes things like ice cream **melt** because it makes the particles they are made of – molecules – move more freely.

Temperature is how hot or cold something is.

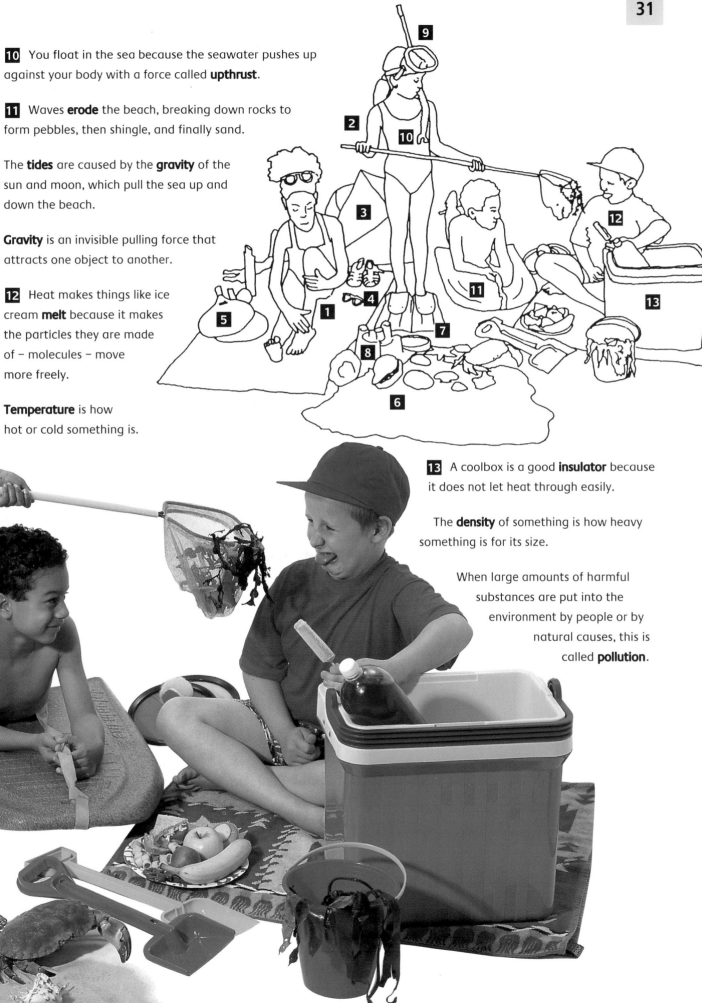

13 A coolbox is a good **insulator** because it does not let heat through easily.

The **density** of something is how heavy something is for its size.

When large amounts of harmful substances are put into the environment by people or by natural causes, this is called **pollution**.

Answers to quizzes

Page

7 **1** True. The kite was 650m long and *Diplodocus* was 27m long; **2** True; **3** False. The tallest are usually only as big as a house.

11 **1** Seagull; **2** Dog; **3** Person; **4** Mouse.

17 **1** False. They have tough stalks (like the necks of barnacle geese) to anchor themselves to any floating debris or boat hulls at sea; **2** False. It is the empty egg case of the lesser spotted dogfish, which is often washed up on the beach; **3** True; **4** True. This is how coconut palm trees have spread and come to grow along many tropical beaches.

27 **1** False. They are full of air, which is lighter than water; **2** True; **3** False; **4** True.

Index